Jeanne d'Albret

The Flight to La Rochelle

1

Table of Contents

Chapter 1: A Narrow Escape — 4

Chapter 2: Childhood and Early Years — 29

Chapter 3: An Ample Declaration — 33

Chapter 4: In a Time Of Prosperity, Prosper! — 44

Chapter 5: Rome's Quiet Conquest — 50

Chapter 6: Jeanne's Bold Proclamation — 62

Chapter 7: A Royal Confrontation, A House Divided — 66

Chapter 8: Times of Trial — 76

Glossary	80
Vocabulary Activities	84
Compare and Contrast Activity	86
Geography Activity	88
Reflection Questions	90
Reflection with Scripture Questions	96

As the hour crept toward midnight, a cool autumn breeze fluttered in through the window of the queen's chamber, stirring the ruby red bed curtains. The fire, answering the wind's whisper, crackled gently and hummed a lullaby into the quiet night. The steady rise and fall of a woman's breath accompanied the tune of the flames, as she dreamed, untroubled and peaceful, wrapped in fine linen sheets that caressed her soft skin.

A Narrow Escape

5

BANG–BANG–BANG!

Jeanne's eyes burst open as her body flew upright from the mattress. Startled, she swiftly tore back the curtains surrounding her bed, and shivered as her bare feet met the cold wooden floor.

"Votre Majesté!" The familiar voice of her **chamberlain** called, echoing urgently through the corridor. Jeanne rushed for the door, cracking it just enough to reveal her face while hiding her **disheveled** attire. 7

"Your majesty–Aire has fallen to Monluc's forces, the **herald** has just arrived; he awaits you in the **salon**."

Forgetting all **propriety**, Jeanne flung the door wide open and beckoned the chamberlain inside. With an averted gaze and blushing cheeks, the gentlemen entered as Jeanne paced frantically in front of the fireplace, her mind spiraling out of control. This was the second city her kingdom had lost to the Catholic forces led by the ruthless Blaise de Monluc in a single month.

"You prepared for this," spoke the Lord's gentle yet commanding voice, quieting the storm of panic that threatened her **resolve**. Jeanne breathed in deeply and released the tormenting thoughts.

"Awaken Henri, have his valets prepare him for the journey to La Rochelle as we planned–and Catherine as well. Send in my handmaidens to dress me and inform the herald that I will see him shortly."

"Of course, madame." Her chamberlain replied, bowing swiftly before turning toward the door.

"Oh, and Piers...ready the horses and see that the royal vaults are emptied and secured for travel," Jeanne uttered softly. Her faithful servant looked back, sorrow clouding his eyes.

"As you wish, madame."

Jeanne dressed promptly and hurried to the salon. Her grey eyes glistened as she sat upon an ivory sofa, folding her hands tightly in her lap. The herald fell to his knees before her as he recounted the events in Aire.

The small and outmatched Huguenot **garrison** stationed at Aire had been struck without mercy. Chaos erupted—many townspeople attempted to flee, some on foot, some atop horses, and some with young children in tow, as the battle raged.

Monluc's assault was swift and brutal. His men made sure every soldier fell under the sword. They **pillaged** the town, took many prisoners, and left nothing but heartbreak and ruin. Many families lost their husbands, brothers, and sons.

Tears streamed down Jeanne's cheeks as the herald finished his report. As queen, she knew that God had entrusted her with the sacred duty to lead, protect, and serve the people of her kingdom. Her heart ached knowing that so many of her subjects were suffering and torn apart by this war.

"Lean into Me Beloved," Christ whispered. Jeanne closed her eyes and prayed silently, reflecting on God's **grief** for humanity and the hardness of His children's hearts. She meditated on Jesus' personal ministry on Earth, and His courage in standing up against the misguided religious and political leaders, to proclaim a message of love and **redemption**. She drew her strength from His example.

"I have not come to bring peace, but a sword." His words echoed through her spirit. This was her mission–to give her people access to God through scripture and personal relationship with Christ, to stand up against those who would prevent His word from being **accessible** to all.

Jeanne sighed and rose from the sofa.

"Go and find my brother, Louis, the Prince de Condé," she said firmly. "Tell him everything you have told me. Tell him that we are departing with the supplies for La Rochelle at this very moment."

The herald nodded and lowered his forehead towards the ground.

"But first," Jeanne added, her voice softening, "go to the kitchens. My servants will see to you. You shall have a warm meal, fresh clothes, and **provisions** for the road–as well as a new horse if it should suit you."

"Thank you, Your Majesty." He replied, taking leave of his Queen. Before Jeanne could draw her next breath, one of her handmaidens entered and curtsied.

"Madame, the children are ready and waiting in the carriage house. The local generals and noblemen loyal to our cause have arrived. They stand prepared to **escort** you, the children, and the royal treasures to La Rochelle."

Jeanne nodded and followed her trusted servant to the carriage house. Her thoughts began to race once more. The road ahead would take nearly a **fortnight**, and be full of danger. With her children and the royal coffers in tow, the company would be forced to move slowly, burdened by the heavy caravans full of jewels, important documents, and other family heirlooms.

The secure passage of these items was vital for the Huguenot cause. The company would need to take secret paths through forested mountains and valleys. The local inhabitants often whispered of these woods being home to shapeshifting entities, witches, wild beasts, werewolves and vampires.

Yet Jeanne feared something far greater– the fallen heart of man and the soldiers and informants loyal to the Catholic cause. On orders from Pope Pious IV, many sought compensation or a monetary reward for delivering her, and her children, over to the Spanish Inquisitors. This war had taken everything from her. Her husband, her lands, the rights of her people to seek God for themselves, and now they were after her life and the lives of her children.

Jeanne knew that following Christ meant giving up many things, but now her courage would be tested more than ever. She straightened her shoulders and whispered a quiet prayer. Whatever dangers laid ahead, she would trust God to guide her through them.

"*What did Peter say when faced with such* **opposition**?" Christ asked.

"We must obey God, rather than man!" Jeanne proclaimed, drawing the attention of her startled handmaiden. She smiled and entered the carriage house. Following God and His word was more important than following the ways of men.

As soon as the queen entered the carriage house, Catherine ran to her mother and clung to her skirts, bursting into tears. Jeanne soothingly stroked her daughter's soft chestnut hair, whispering words of comfort. The past few years had been difficult on Catherine. The family had been forced to relocate multiple times, fleeing from many enemies that were trying to arrest Jeanne and seize control over her son Henri, heir to the Kingdom of Navarre.

"Don't worry Mother, I will protect you and Catherine from any danger we encounter on the road!" Henri proclaimed boldly. He would be fifteen in a few months, and had grown so rapidly over the past year that many at court affectionately referred to him as the resident giant. Henri was becoming a skilled and brave soldier, training daily with the Huguenot forces and under the supervision of his Uncle Louis.

"Of course you will, my brave prince." Jeanne smiled, kissing her son affectionately on his cheek. Outside, the courtyard bustled with quiet movement—soldiers adjusting their saddles, servants fastening trunks, and horses snorting loudly in the cool morning. The air smelled of damp earth and leather.

A uniformed soldier approached on horseback, sitting tall in his saddle. "We're ready, Madame," he said. "Everything is secured, and the royal carriage is awaiting you and the princess. Prince Henri, your horse has been prepared."

"Yes. Thank you, commander."

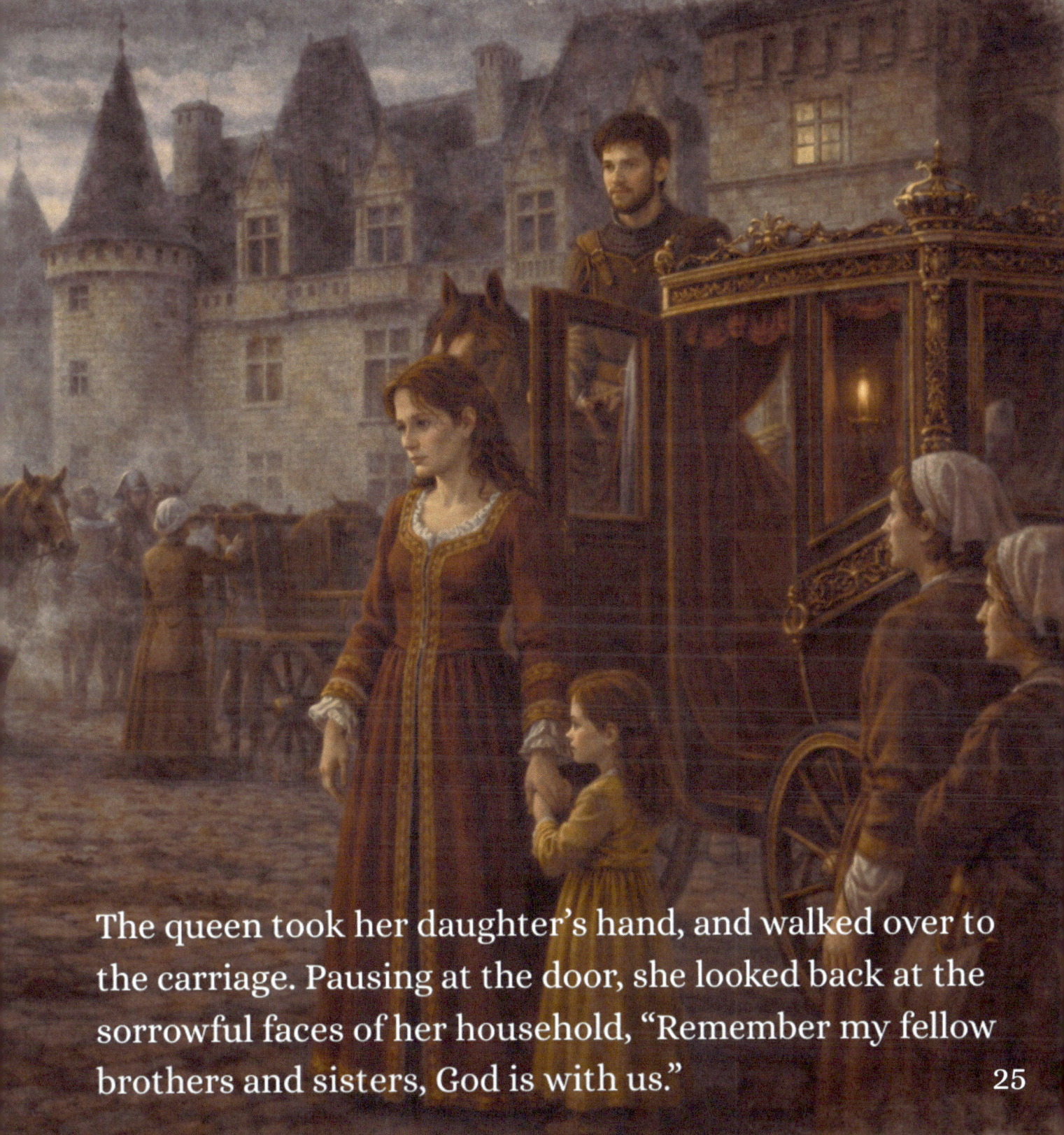

The queen took her daughter's hand, and walked over to the carriage. Pausing at the door, she looked back at the sorrowful faces of her household, "Remember my fellow brothers and sisters, God is with us."

25

Henri mounted his horse swiftly. The majestic brown stallion trotted gracefully amidst the chaos before halting outside the royal carriage. "I'll be here, riding alongside this wooden beast, should you need anything," he said, knocking humorously on the wooden caravan. Jeanne nodded thankfully.

Suddenly, the driver flicked the reins, and the horses began to move. Wheels creaked, hooves struck the cobblestones, and the small **convoy** set out into the morning mist. As the town of Tardes disappeared behind them, Jeanne whispered a prayer beneath her breath. "Father, send your spirit before us, be our shield, our protector, and our light upon the road to La Rochelle. In Jesus name, Amen."

Childhood and Early Years

Long ago, in a bustling suburb of Saint-Germain-en-Laye, just outside the city of Paris, a baby girl was born on November 16th, 1528. Her name was Jeanne. Her parents, King Henri and Queen Marguerite of Navarre, were kind and thoughtful rulers who were loved by their people. They cared for the poor, encouraged learning, and provided a safe place to live for people who were treated unfairly because of their faith. Navarre became known as a **refuge** for Protestants seeking peace.

29

Jeanne grew up in a world filled with new ideas and lively conversation. She was surrounded by scholars, **reformers**, and philosophers, who gathered to talk about faith and new ways of understanding God's Word. She always listened to these conversations carefully, her bright eyes shining with curiosity.

Jeanne often asked her tutor questions about the scriptures and the world. Their conversations shaped her quick wit and independent thinking. Like her mother, she believed that every person should be able to read the scriptures and know Christ personally through faith, bible study, and prayer, rather than relying on priests, rituals, and traditions.

Even as a child, Jeanne's heart belonged to God, and her free spirit would one day change the course of her kingdom.

An Ample Declaration

One afternoon, Marguerite and Henri came into the drawing room to find their daughter, Jeanne, stretched out across the floor with a leather bound book in front of her. Propped up on her elbows, she closely examined the text, tracing each line with her finger.

"Jeanne." The strong voice of her father called.

"Papa!" She cried leaping into the air. She ran into her father's warm embrace. He hugged her tightly and spun her around before gently setting her feet back onto the floor.

"Jeanne, we have something we must tell you." Her mother spoke softly, "Come and sit down for a moment."

Jeanne nodded and plopped down on the sofa, next to her mother.

"The King, that is your Uncle Francis," Marguerite spoke, holding her daughter's hands, "He has decided, with an unchanging mind, that you are to marry Duke Wilhelm of Cleves from Germany."

Jeanne's happy **countenance** fell, as her eyes shifted rapidly back and forth, studying the regretful expressions of her mother and father, searching for any sign of their resistance to this **absurd** proposal.

Finding none, she burst into tears, "Absolutely not! Mother–I am much too young! This is disgraceful! How can you allow this?"

"It's been decided Jeanne. We aren't happy about it but it's been decided." Henri said firmly.

35

Jeanne threw herself on the floor and wailed loudly. "Traitors! All of you!"

"My love–" Marguerite began, falling to the floor in an effort to comfort her daughter.

"No!" Jeanne shouted, batting her mother's hands away. "I will write a letter of protest to the King this instant! He cannot force me into such an unholy union."

Jeanne ran to the desk in the drawing room, pulled out some parchment and immediately began to scribble out her protest.

37

I, Jeanne de Navarre, do hereby affirm and protest, that the marriage which is being contracted between the Duke of Cleves and myself is against my will; that I have never consented to it, nor will consent; and that whatever words may be drawn from me in the days to come, let it be known they are spoken under force, stolen from my lips by fear—fear of the King, my father, and of the Queen, my mother, who has threatened to have me punished by my governess if I do not comply!

As the days before her wedding approached, Jeanne felt her faith in God begin to waver. How could He allow His beloved daughter to face such a dreadful fate? How could He abandon her when she needed Him the most? Why had He not answered her prayers and **intervened** on her behalf?

"Where are You?" She whispered desperately into the darkness of each night with tears streaming down her sticky cheeks. But no answer ever came.

Despite her passionate protests and pleas to the Lord, Jeanne was forcibly married to Wilhelm, Duke of Cleves, in June 1541. However, her parents managed to persuade the French King to allow their young daughter to remain at home until she reached maturity. Her new husband departed for his court in Germany, and Jeanne stayed safely with her family in France.

41

With holy **conviction**, Queen Marguerite devised a letter writing campaign to free her daughter from this unwanted marriage. Marguerite wrote frequent letters to her brother, the King of France, arguing for the annulment of the marriage. Meanwhile, Jeanne sent polite letters to her husband, Duke Wilhelm, with news of her daily life, and simple expressions of admiration, though her heart was never his. They kept up their letter scheme for years, trusting that in God's timing their efforts would be fruitful.

At last, in 1545, King Francis agreed to allow the Pope to **annul** the marriage, recognizing that it had been forced and that Jeanne had never left France to live or share a life with her husband. Her fervent prayers had finally been answered. From that moment on, Jeanne knew that God was her strength and her rock during her sufferings, and that He would be with her through every uncertain and frightening time.

In 1547, King Francis I passed away, and his son, King Henri II, took the throne. Although her father wished to marry her to Prince Philip of Spain, her cousin, holding much more authority than the King of Navarre, decided to wed her to Antoine de Bourbon, Duke of Vendome. Jeanne welcomed the match with an open heart. Antoine was charming, dashing, and courageous. He was also an excellent soldier and military general, respected by all. Most importantly, he was known to be a friend of the Huguenot cause, which pleased Jeanne deeply, as well as her family and her companions.

In a Time Of Prosperity, Prosper!

45

The first years of Jeanne and Antoine's marriage were filled with happiness. Together, they traveled back and forth between the grand courts of France and the peaceful valleys of Bearn. Wherever they went, people greeted them with cheers and blessings. They were an attractive pair, both young, free-spirited, and full of hope for the future.

Antoine loved adventure and the thrill of battle. He often rode off with his brother's soldiers, and Jeanne would write long devotional letters to her husband whenever he was away, filled with scripture and prayers for his safety. He always returned with stories of bravery and victory that delighted her. With each passing day their bond grew stronger—to many it seemed **impenetrable**.

On December 14th, 1553, the couple's joy was complete when their son was born — Henri, the future King of Navarre and Henri IV of France. Antoine was proud beyond measure, boasting that their child would one day bring peace to France. As soon as Jeanne's eyes opened each morning, she praised God for the blessings He had bestowed upon her.

One afternoon Jeanne, Antoine, and little Henri lounged under the summer sun in the palace gardens after a picnic lunch. A few hours earlier, they had attended a Protestant service, and the joy of worship still lingered in their hearts. With a stomach full of delicious food, Antoine dozed peacefully with his head in Jeanne's lap. She ran her fingers gently through her husband's hair while baby Henri slept soundly in his basket beside her. Jeanne closed her eyes in this blissful moment to whisper a quiet prayer.

"Father, thank You for this beautiful afternoon. Thank You for my family and for every blessing You have given me."

In the stillness of her soul, she felt her Savior's gentle reply, "Enjoy these moments with your family, Jeanne. Trials will come—but remember, I will be with you through them all."

Jeanne's eyes flew open. "Antoine!" she cried suddenly, startling her husband, who sat up at once. Overcome with a strange urgency, she took his face in her hands. "Antoine, promise me—promise me right now that nothing will ever tear us apart. That nothing will ever come between us or separate us."

"*Ma belle,* our love can conquer anything. Don't worry." Antoine replied, before leaning closer to offer his bride a comforting kiss.

Rome's Quiet Conquest

In 1555, Jeanne and Antoine became Queen and King of Navarre. The royal couple continued Henri and Marguerite's practice of religious tolerance, but chose to attend Protestant services rather than Catholic mass. Many in the kingdom followed their example, inspired by their courage and faith. The Huguenots often gathered quietly in open fields, barns or private homes at dawn or sunset to avoid unwanted attention from Catholic authorities and loyalists. These small meetings closely resembled the gatherings of the early Christians.

Together, the people sang psalms from Pseaumes Octante Trois de David—The Eighty-Three Psalms of David. After the singing, a literate member of the group would stand to read from the scriptures in French and share a sermon based on the Scripture. The service ended with the congregation praying together, united in faith and hope.

As summer approached, Jeanne and Antoine were filled with joy when they learned that Jeanne was expecting another child. They decided to return to Paris for the season so they could share the happy news with the royal court. Now five years old, their son Henri was growing quickly, and it was time to find suitable tutors to begin his studies.

One warm Friday evening, Jeanne and Antoine joined a social gathering in the great hall of the French court. The large room glimmered in the candlelight . Silk banners hung from the walls, and the air was thick with perfume, laughter, and the hum of conversation. Antoine stood tall and proud, in the center of it all, surrounded by courtiers in crimson and gold.

Despite the growing tensions between the Catholics and the supporters of the Huguenots, these noble and elite families always managed to engage in a civilized dance of **pretension**, deception, and criticism disguised with flowery words and concerned tones.

Jeanne stood near the fireplace, gently stroking her belly, and watched her husband carefully. Members of King Philip's court surrounded the King of Navarre like vultures. She had no doubt they were trying to convince him to return to the Catholic faith. Antonie's brother had recently declared **fidelity** to the Huguenot cause, as leader and military general for the Protestant forces. This had angered many at court, who were determined to make Jeanne and Antoine end their practice of religious tolerance in their kingdom.

"You are a man born for greatness, Your Majesty," the Duke said, his voice carrying just enough for Jeanne to hear. "The King trusts you. The Queen Mother admires your courage. And Spain — ah, Spain would welcome the rightful King of Navarre, if only he stood with the true faith once more."

Jeanne's breath caught. She saw the flicker of hunger in Antoine's eyes, the same spark that had once drawn her to him, the twinkle of a brave knight. The courtiers murmured vows of praise and promise. Their words of unity, power, wealth, glory, God's true will–all dangled before Antoine like bright jewels. She could see the stars forming in his eyes and her heart fell.

Later that night, Jeanne found Antoine alone near the window, staring out into the dark gardens. "They mean to turn you from the truth," she said in soft confrontation.

Antoine turned to her, his expression weary. "They mean to restore what is ours. Think of it, Jeanne — Navarre united again! Our son a true prince and ruler of both lands!"

Jeanne shook her head, tears glistening in her eyes. "At what cost, Antoine? Will you trade God's assignment, His truth, for the promises of men?"

He hesitated, unable to meet her gaze. "I must think of our future and the future of our son," he whispered.

"Our future lies in the Lord's hands, you know that Antoine," Jeanne said. But her words seemed to fade into the night.

When Antoine left the next morning to attend mass with the royal court, Jeanne remained behind in prayer. She stood in still silence before the Lord and whispered, tears streaming down her cheeks,

"Even if all others forsake You, I will not."

A fortnight passed, and Antoine continued to attend Catholic mass, despite Jeanne's pleas and protests. The stress of his return to Catholicism became unbearable, and for the sake of her unborn child, she withdrew from life at court, and retired to quieter calmer surroundings. She left her son Henri in the care of his father so that she could focus on a peaceful pregnancy.

On February 7th, 1559, the princess of Navarre was born, Catherine de Bourbon. Jeanne and Antoine rejoiced in the safe arrival of their daughter, even as uncertainty clouded their marriage and tension grew between the couple.

With two children to secure his legacy, Antoine grew more determined than ever to restore the Kingdom of Navarre to what he believed was its former glory. In pursuit of power and royal favor, he continued to support the Catholic faith, a choice that would widen the divide between him and Jeanne.

Jeanne's Bold Proclamation

Meanwhile, Jeanne found comfort and guidance through her frequent exchange of letters with John Calvin, a leading voice of the Protestant Reformation, and the founder of Calvinism. His words strengthened her faith and helped shape her understanding of scripture. On Christmas Day in 1560, Jeanne publicly declared herself a Calvinist. She ended the **policy** of religious tolerance in Navarre, closed the monasteries and convents, and required all priests and nuns to leave the kingdom. Catholic rituals were no longer permitted in Navarre.

63

Like her mother, Marguerite, Jeanne believed deeply that every person should be able to read and understand God's Word. She continued her mother's mission to bring scripture to the Kingdom of Navarre by **facilitating** and financing the translation of the New Testament into Basque and Bearnese.

She wanted everyone, no matter what language they spoke, to study God's words for themselves rather than relying only on ritual or a priest to **mediate** the relationship. She wanted to strengthen the sound of His voice in their hearts. To make this possible, Jeanne also supported literacy programs, helping her people learn to read so they could study the Bible in their own language.

65

A Royal Confrontation, A House Divided

Jeanne's new religious policies in Navarre added fuel to the growing tensions between the Huguenots and Catholics across France. Until finally, the conflict erupted into violence. On the morning of March 6th, 1562, Jeanne received word that a massacre had taken place during a Protestant worship service, in the small town of Wassy, east of Paris, five days earlier. The Catholics, led by the Duke of Guise, stormed the building, while the worshipers were singing psalms to the Lord. Many tried to escape through a hole in the roof, but were met with gunfire from **sharpshooters** as they fled.

Upon hearing the news, Jeanne immediately called for the leading military general for the Huguenot cause and her brother by marriage, Louis de Bourbon. The two conversed in agony, knowing that the time had come where much innocent blood would be spilled for religious freedom. Suddenly, their conversation was interrupted by a loud banging on the door.

The chamber was heavy with silence when Antoine entered. His boots echoed against the stone floor, each step sharp and hurried. Jeanne stood near the window, her hands folded calmly before her, while Louis, Antoine's brother, remained at her side.

"You both have gone too far," Antoine said at last, his voice rigid. "Your actions are tearing our kingdom apart and isolating us from our allies in France. The King of Spain and the Pope are on the verge of calling for your imprisonment!"

Jeanne turned to face him, her chin lifted. "I am only following the assignment God gave me, an assignment that you once believed in with all your heart," she replied sorrowfully. "I cannot deny what I know to be true."

Antoine's eyes flickered in rage. "This is no longer about whatever you think God told you," he snapped, "Is God the author of violence? France is now torn apart by civil war because of this madness."

69

"A civil war sparked by a rogue Catholic militia—led by your new friend, the Duke of Guise," Louis said sharply. "Tell me, brother, what drove these so-called righteous men to storm a peaceful worship service and murder fifty Protestants, including women and even a child?"

Antoine ignored him. "I have declared myself for the Catholic cause—for peace and for order," he said firmly. "And as your husband and head, I demand that you do the same."

"I will not," Jeanne said, her voice steady though her heart pounded. "I will not disobey God and pledge fidelity to Rome."

Antoine stepped closer, his fists clenched. "You will obey me. You are my wife."

Before Jeanne could speak, Louis moved forward. "That's enough," he said firmly, placing himself between them.

Antoine turned sharply. "This does not concern you brother."

"It concerns me when my sister is threatened," Louis replied. "And it concerns all people who seek the freedom to worship God without fear."

Antoine scoffed. "You will lead her into danger."

"She has chosen faith over fear," Louis continued. "You ask her to surrender her soul for tradition—but an empire, holy or not, built on lies will never last. Tradition that defies the Word of God will crumble."

"Spirit and truth–that's what our Lord said, don't you remember, my love?" Jeanne nearly whispered, stepping forward and gently placing her hands on her husband's cheeks. The ache in her heart grew as she searched for any sign of the man she once knew.

The room fell silent. Antoine looked deeply into his wife's tearful eyes– her resolve would not bend.

"I see," he said regretfully. "You have made your choice then."

Without another word, Antoine turned and left the chamber. Jeanne exhaled, her knees trembling until she collapsed into the arms of her brother-in-law, weeping.

"You are not alone," he said. "And you never will be. If God is for us, who can be against us?"

Jeanne nodded, drawing strength from her brother's words. Whatever lay ahead, she knew that her love for Christ would give her the courage, strength, and faith she needed to fight for humanity's right to hear His words and worship freely.

"I know it's difficult, Jeanne, but I came to bring a sword, not peace. I am with you." Her Savior's voice whispered like a gentle breeze in her heart.

That very afternoon, Jeanne left Paris in **haste**. With a heavy heart, she was forced to leave her son Henri behind as she returned to Navarre alongside Louis, who had gathered loyal men to escort them on the journey.

Along the way, unrest broke out, and groups of Protestants attacked Catholic churches, tearing down icons and statues that they believed dishonored God.

When Antoine learned of this, his anger flared. He ordered the arrest of both his wife and his brother. He dispatched troops to seize Jeanne and bring her back to Paris, where he planned to confine her to a convent under armed guard.

Jeanne, however, reached Bearn safely. Once home, she acted quickly and **fortified** the kingdom against invasion. To support the Huguenot cause, she sold some of her jewelry, treasured family heirlooms, and other valuables, using the funds to help protect her people and their faith.

Times of Trial

One cool autumn evening in October 1562, Jeanne received heartbreaking news. Her husband, Antoine, had been mortally wounded in battle at Rouen. Desperate to see him one last time, she tried to arrange for her safe passage across enemy lines so she could nurse him back to health. But it was too late. Antoine died far from her side.

Grief-stricken, Jeanne focused her attention on retrieving her young son, Henri. She returned to Paris and began **negotiating** with Catherine de' Medici, queen-regent of France. Finally in 1566, she convinced Catherine to allow the future King of Navarre to return to his lands. At last mother and son were reunited, and the two returned to their homelands of Bearn.

With the help of his Uncle Louis, Henri was raised to be a **staunch** supporter of the Huguenot cause and future leader of the Huguenot forces. With the death of Antoine, Louis became a source of strength for Jeanne and her children. The family spent many years moving around different regions of Bearn, evading Catholic forces, and others who wished to turn them over to the Spanish Inquisitors or Rome. Finally, when the third war of religion broke out in 1568, the family settled in the Protestant stronghold of La Rochelle. Sadly, tragedy struck the family again when Louis was captured and **executed** in the Battle of Jarnac on March 16th, 1569.

Even after this loss, Jeanne remained brave, determined, and rooted firmly in Christ. She continued her God-given mission to make sure the people of her kingdom could read the Bible in their native languages, and she persisted in fighting for religious freedom and the right to worship without fear. Her steadfast love and loyalty to Jesus Christ, made it possible for her to continue her goal of bringing the Kingdom of Heaven to Earth.

79

Glossary

1. **chamberlain:** (p. 7) a trusted royal servant who helped manage the queen's household and delivered important messages
2. **disheveled:** (p. 7) messy or untidy, especially in appearance or clothing
3. **herald:** (p. 8) an official messenger who carried important news, often for a king or queen
4. **salon:** (p. 8) a large room used for meetings or receiving important guests
5. **propriety:** (p. 8) proper behavior; acting in a way that is polite and socially acceptable
6. **resolve:** (p. 10) strong determination to do something, even when it is difficult
7. **garrison:** (p. 13) a group of soldiers stationed in a town or fortress to protect it
8. **pillaged:** (p. 13) to steal or destroy goods violently, usually during war

9. **grief:** (p. 14) deep sadness, especially after loss or tragedy
10. **redemption:** (p. 14) being saved or forgiven
11. **accessible:** (p. 14) easy to reach, use, or understand
12. **provisions:** (p. 17) supplies such as food, clothing, and equipment needed for a journey
13. **escort:** (p. 18) to protect and travel with someone to keep them safe
14. **fortnight:** (p. 18) a period of two weeks
15. **opposition:** (p. 21) people or forces that resist or fight against something
16. **convoy:** (p. 27) a group traveling together for safety, often with guards or soldiers
17. **refuge:** (p. 29) a safe place where people can go to escape danger
18. **reformers:** (p. 30) people who worked to change the church and improve religious practices

Glossary

19. **countenance:** (p. 34) a person's facial or body expression
20. **absurd:** (p. 34) completely unreasonable or silly
21. **intervened:** (p. 40) stepped in to change a situation or help stop a problem
22. **conviction:** (p. 43) a strong belief that someone has
23. **annul:** (p. 43) to officially cancel something, such as a marriage
24. **impenetrable:** (p. 46) impossible to break through or separate
25. **pretension:** (p. 53) false or exaggerated behavior meant to impress others
26. **fidelity:** (p. 53) faithfulness and loyalty to a person, cause, or belief
27. **policy:** (p. 62) an official plan or rule made by a government or leader
28. **facilitating:** (p. 65) helping make something possible or easier

29. **mediate:** (p. 65) to act as a go-between to help people understand or communicate
30. **sharpshooters:** (p. 66) highly skilled soldiers trained to shoot accurately from a distance
31. **haste:** (p. 74) great speed or urgency
32. **fortified:** (p. 75) strengthened or protected against attack
33. **negotiating:** (p. 76) trying to reach an agreement through discussion
34. **staunch:** (p. 77) very loyal and strongly committed
35. **executed:** (p. 77) put to death as a punishment

Vocabulary Activities

Vocabulary Art Studio
- Choose 3–5 vocabulary words
- For each word:
  - Write the word and definition
  - Draw a picture showing the meaning in the story
  - Explain your artwork out loud to a parent, sibling, teacher, or friend

Memory Match (DIY Game)

- Write vocabulary words on one set of cards
- Write definitions on another set of cards
- Place them face down and play by matching pairs

Compare and Contrast Activity

Step 1: Make Your Journal
- Fold a piece of paper in half
- Write the title: Life in the Mid-1500s France vs. Now across the top of the page

Step 2: Life in Jeanne's Time
- On the first half, draw or write about life in the 1500s. Think about:
  - Traveling by horse, carriage, or convoy
  - Sending messages by herald or letter
  - Worshiping in secret because it was dangerous
  - Clothing people wore and daily routines

Step 3: Compare to Life Today

- On the second half, draw or write about life today
- Compare and contrast with these ideas:
  - How we travel now
  - How we communicate
  - Freedom to worship
  - Safety and comfort

Step 4: Think and Reflect

- On the back of the paper answer this question:
  - Which part of Jeanne's life would have been the hardest for you? Why?

Geography Activity

Materials
- Blank outline map of France
- Colored pencils, crayons, or watercolor paints
- Pencil & eraser
- Ruler
- Atlas or computer

Step 1: Map Setup
- Title the map at the top: Jeanne d'Albret's Journey to La Rochelle (1568)
- Label key locations: Tarbes– where Jeanne began her flight, Béarn – her homeland, La Rochelle – Protestant stronghold and destination
- Optional challenge: Label nearby regions, mountain ranges or rivers

Step 2: Plotting the Journey

- Draw the travel route using pencil
- Use a dashed line to show secret or hidden travel paths
- Avoid major cities when possible to show how Jeanne tried to stay safe

Step 3: Artistic Symbols

- Add symbols along the route to represent historical challenges
- Suggested Symbols
  - ⚔️ Crossed swords → Danger / Catholic forces
  - 🌲 Trees → Forests used for hiding
  - ⛰️ Mountains → Difficult terrain
  - 🛡️ Shield → Escort or protection
  - ✝️ Cross → Worship or faith
- Create a Map Key / Legend in a corner explaining each symbol

89

Geography Activity

Step 4: Aging the Map (Optional but Fun!)
- Lightly brush the paper with cooled tea or coffee using a sponge
- Let it dry completely
- Gently crumple and flatten the edges

Color the Map
- Use crayons, colored pencils, or watercolors to color the map

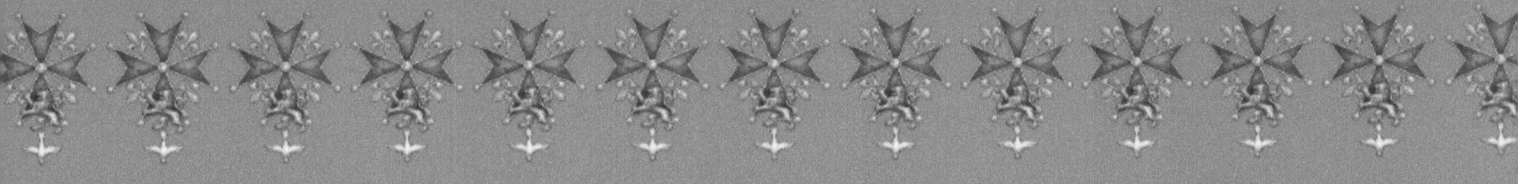

Step 5: Written Reflection (Choose One)
- Write 5-8 sentences answering ONE prompt:
  - Why was this journey dangerous?
  - What part of the journey would have frightened you most?

Courage When Faith Is Tested

Courage is not the absence of fear—it is choosing faith even while afraid. Jeanne showed courage when she stood firm in her beliefs, even when powerful people opposed her. Her bravery reminds us that faith sometimes requires standing out from those around you.

Reflect:

- How did Jeanne show courage during dangerous moments in her life?
- What does courage look like for someone your age today?
- When have you had to be brave for what you believe is right?

Obedience to God's Calling

Jeanne believed God had given her a mission: to help people know His Word. Even when others tried to stop her, she remained obedient. Obedience means listening to God's voice, even when other voices are louder.

Reflect:

- Why was it important to Jeanne that people could read the Bible for themselves?
- How did Jeanne use her position as queen to serve God and others?
- What gifts or responsibilities has God given you that you can use to serve others?

Persevering Through Loss and Opposition

Jeanne experienced deep loss—her husband, her brother-in-law, the lives of her people, and her safety. Still, she did not give up. She turned her grief into strength and allowed God to carry her through sorrow. Perseverance means continuing forward, even when the heart is heavy.

Reflect:

- How do you think Jeanne found strength after losing people she loved?
- Why is it difficult to follow God when others disagree or oppose us?
- What helps you keep going when something feels unfair or painful?

Faith Over Fear & the Gift of Freedom

Jeanne believed faith was worth more than comfort or safety. Because of people like her, many today can worship freely. Her story reminds us that freedom often comes through sacrifice and faithfulness.

Reflect:

- Why do you think Jeanne chose faith over safety?
- Why is religious freedom important to protect?
- How can Jeanne's faith encourage you to live boldly for God today?

Reflection with Scripture

Read Acts 5:29 TLV Peter and the emissaries replied, "We must obey God rather than men."

- Jeanne chose to obey God even when powerful leaders pressured her to turn away from her faith. She believed God's truth mattered more than human approval or safety. How does this verse explain the choices Jeanne made when others tried to control her faith?

- Have you ever felt pressured to do something you knew was not right? How can this verse help you choose obedience to God?

Read Matthew 5:10 TLV Blessed are those who have been persecuted for the sake of righteousness, for theirs is the kingdom of heaven.

- Jeanne suffered loss, danger, and rejection because she stood up for what she believed was right. Even in hardship, she trusted that God saw her faithfulness. What hardships did Jeanne face because of her faith?

- Have you ever been treated unfairly for doing the right thing? How might God use those moments to strengthen you?

Reflection with Scripture

Read Psalm 46:2 TLV God is our refuge and strength, an ever-present help in trouble.

- When Jeanne had no safe place to turn, she relied on God as her refuge. Through prayer and faith, she found strength even while on the run. How was God a refuge for Jeanne and her children during dangerous times?

- When you feel afraid or overwhelmed, how can you turn to God as your refuge?

Read Joshua 1:9 TLV "Have I not commanded you? Chazak! Be strong! Do not be terrified or dismayed, for Adonai your God is with you wherever you go."

- Jeanne showed courage when she fled danger, protected her children, and stood firm in her beliefs —even when she felt afraid. Where do you see Jeanne choosing courage instead of fear?

- What is a situation in your life where God might be calling you to be brave and trust that He is with you?

Reflection with Scripture

Read John 10:27 TLV My sheep hear My voice. I know them, and they follow Me.

- Throughout her life, Jeanne learned to listen for God's voice, especially in moments of fear and confusion. When others tried to guide her with promises of safety, power, or approval, Jeanne chose to follow what she believed God was asking of her. She trusted that God knew her heart and would lead her in the right direction. Like a shepherd guiding his sheep, God gently directed Jeanne step by step, even when the path was dangerous.

- How did Jeanne show that she was listening to God's voice instead of the voices around her?

- What tools or spiritual practices helped Jeanne understand whether or not she was hearing God's voice?

- What are some ways you can listen for God's voice in your own life?

- Why is reading scripture so important for discerning God's voice?

Reflection with Scripture

Read Jeremiah 29:12-13 TLV Then you will call on Me, and come and pray to Me, and I will listen to you. You will seek Me and find Me, when you will search for Me with all your heart.

- Jeanne did not see God as distant or unreachable. She prayed, reflected, and sought Him with her whole heart. Even while fleeing danger and facing loss, she believed God was listening to her prayers. Jeanne's relationship with God gave her strength, comfort, and purpose. She knew that God was not only her King, but also her refuge and friend.

- How does your relationship with God give you strength, comfort, and purpose?

- How does your life display God's kingship?

- What does it look like for you to seek God with your whole heart, even in small, everyday moments?

- If someone is looking to find God, what advice would you give them to help direct their steps towards Him?

Tarbes, Béarn, France

Little House in Heaven
© April Marie Utile